BE WHO YOU ARE

Jean Klein, a musicologist and doctor from Central Europe, spent his early years inquiring about the essence of life. He had the inner conviction that there was a 'principle' independent of all society and felt the urge to explore this conviction.

His exploration led him to India where he was introduced through a 'direct approach' to the non-mental dimension of life. Through living in this complete openness, he was taken, one timeless moment, by a sudden, clear awakening in his real nature. It was not a mystical experience, a new state, but the continuum in life, the non-state in light of which birth, death and all experience take place.

From 1960 he led a quiet life teaching in Europe and later in the United States.

BE WHO YOU ARE

Jean Klein

Translated by Mary Mann

NON-DUALITY PRESS

Jean Klein Foundation
PO Box 22045
Santa Barbara, CA 93120
United States

jkftmp@aol.com
http://www.jean klein.org

Cover illustration: *Gedächtnisbild für JE Bremer*
by Casper David Friedrich

ISBN 978-0-9551762-5-8

Non-Duality Press
6 Folkestone Rd, Salisbury SP2 8JP
United Kingdom
www.non-dualitybooks.com

I

During these meetings we shall discuss the knowledge of our true nature. But the word knowledge will here be used in its strict meaning of metaphysical realization, in other words, the actual establishing of ourselves in that which we truly are. It is therefore a total achievement.

This activity implies the absence of any preconceived idea. We do not strive to reach an imaginable goal, because the unknown can be neither imagined nor conceived. In matters of ordinary understanding, one makes use of analogy and reasoning. But here we shall be concerned with a formless absolute, an Ultimate Subject which can never be an object to be apprehended by the mind. Such research obviously implies that it be undertaken empty-handed, by a mind which has rejected the strategy of functioning with the already known. The projection of a "God", a "Self", a "where", a "when", are part of such a strategy and must be entirely laid aside. The only technique – if I may say so – which we can use, is based on an art of listening which is the supreme teaching of the traditional method.

Consequently, our meetings will provide neither information nor documentation in the usual sense of these words. We therefore suggest that no notes be taken. What is important is for you to take up a passively-active attitude. This will enable you to convert into your own substance what such an attitude has allowed you to absorb. You should therefore listen with intense awareness and moreover strive to listen to yourself at the same time.

The ordinary man's activity is made up of reactions which are the expression of his egotistic make-up. He is a self surrounded by pleasant or unpleasant, friendly or hostile objects, and everything which impinges on him incites him to react according to his desires and his fears. Consequently, all his reactions are false, fragmentary, inadequate, because they are rooted in his egotistic outlook which is born of his delusion that he is a separate self. All the traditional doctrines teach us methods by which we may come to discard this state of reaction and reach an ego-less state where all reactions cease to be, giving place to impersonal actions which are true, impartial and adequate.

It may happen that even the egotistic man, under certain circumstances, responds to the challenge of outside objects in such a spontaneous and adequate manner. It does happen at times, when he comes face-to-face with something absolutely new, with something which it is impossible for him to integrate into his egotistical mental framework. It may also happen in the course of a poetical or aesthetic experience, because a thing of beauty, being an expression of harmony, possesses of its own nature a harmonizing power which, placing us temporarily in a state of perfect balance, allows us to be in tune with Reality. But they are few and evanescent, these states of grace, which allow us to catch sight of the lost Paradise, and they remain unnoticed and unpursued because the ego rejects and shuns them, sensing in them a herald of its death.

All this must be thoroughly understood if one wishes to listen to a traditional teaching with any profit. In the presence of a master, the listening should be modelled on the above mentioned "state of grace", during which, for an instant, we may have emerged from the egotistic condition. An effort should be made to remember such states of nakedness, austerity, openness and clarity.

This state of listening is the first true step on the path.

Next we must undertake the observation of our desires so as to understand what it is that we are really seeking in all the objects which seem to please our appetites. We shall then realize that when the desired object is stripped of all its peculiarities, its distinctive characteristics, there remains a constant residue which is the true object of our search and which may be called fullness, bliss and peace. Now it so happens that nothing in the world of objects possesses perfect fullness, nor unconditional bliss. After the conquest of a desired object, we experience a few short moments of non-desire, but very soon desire reappears, and we embark on a new search.

This clearly indicates that what we really desire is not the object, because if it were, its possession would eliminate all desire. What is desired is bliss, *Ananda*, which exists at all times in myself and in everything. The realization of the presence of this bliss was lost to me when I became a separate ego, thereby losing sight of my essential identity with it. From that moment on, the world of objects and duality was born. This duality makes it impossible for us to perceive the presence of this bliss which abides in ourselves as in all things. We can only perceive it in those objects which are more or less in accordance with our egotistic make-up. We are thus compelled to strive in a world where the pleasant and the unpleasant, where good and evil, oppose each other. Most of the time we are content to waver between pleasant-pleasure and unpleasant-pain, having no inkling of that true joy of which pleasure is only a shadow. But it may happen in certain cases, that we find ourselves face to face with an object which is in exceptional harmony with us. We may then transcend pleasure and experience joy; and discover that perfect joy lies beyond the pleasure-pain duality and is of another nature. Indeed pleasure is of its own nature fickle and transitory, hence its fleeting and disappointing character. When it reaches a very high degree of intensity and purity, it may do more than allay desire, it may completely satisfy it. . . for one moment. . . then it gives place to joy. This joy only arises with the suppression of desire, that is, of the ego. This is why true joy is impersonal, is beyond the ego. When we are immersed in perfect joy, we cease to be ourselves, only joy remains, and the object has disappeared with the subject.

I would like to look closely at certain points with

you, points which I have only outlined, but please bear in mind that our study shall be chiefly made up of suggestions, since over-clear and over-precise formulae might be an impediment to any inclination you might have of seeing a question through to its end.

Question
There are two questions I wish to put. The first concerns me personally, the second is of a more general nature. You said we should not take notes and nevertheless I have done so. As time goes by, the more I listen to you and almost unknown to myself, the more do I take up a position of standing aloof. But to obtain a direct contact, to plunge into ultimate reality, it seems to me that one must necessarily make use of the intellect. It is the intellect that views the path, or at least, he thinks he views it. He knows that intellect must be finally eliminated, or at least he thinks be knows it, and that is why it seems to me, that by taking notes of a few essential ideas, on reading them over and being, so to speak, impregnated by them, I get a better result than a direct dive into the unknown.

That is my first question. The second is this: you said at the outset that the search is carried out without searching. What then are we to think of those disciplines intended to condition us in some particular view of an approach to reality?

Answer
To understand this search, we must first rid ourselves of one foregone conclusion, that is, the idea that objects

exist independently of he who perceives them. Next, it must be understood that a simultaneous perception of several objects is impossible.

When we observe something attentively, consciousness penetrates vision and we are nothing else but vision. When we really listen to something, we are nothing else but hearing. We can never be both hearing and seeing simultaneously. We can pass very rapidly from one activity to another, from one thought to another, but absolute simultaneousness is impossible. Thus you can see for yourself that it is impossible to be thoroughly aware of any inner upsurge and take notes at the same time. This cannot but impair the quality of your listening. The word of the master must be seized with its import of the moment, intended to reach the hearer of that moment. The words read over in a page of notes have lost all their initial impact.

As to intellectual preparation, it should be unconditionally discarded, in order that the hearing lose nothing of its authenticity and spontaneity.

Disciplines also should be deliberately set aside, since they necessarily imply compulsion: there is always someone who wants to discipline and something which resists, so that there is always a state of effort and conflict. Before undertaking any profound search, one must be able to look into oneself. One must not however analyse oneself, compare or judge, but one must observe oneself as one would any object. If one attentively observes the inner welling-up, one is thereby absolutely and adequately situated and there is no conflict. Discipline is of no use whatsoever, since things are naturally eliminated by discernment without it being necessary for us to treat them brutally. Even in the course of the technique known as "letting-go", a faint shadow of discipline is implied, for letting-go of an object implies a certain discipline. Only an effortless and choiceless, I repeat *choiceless* reaction, is the hallmark of liberation.

If I understand you rightly, choosing always means remaining in oneself by a voluntary fixation. So that choosing an object is finally choosing oneself whereas by not choosing one is inserted in the totality of life, that totality where all objects merge into one.

Yes, it is by not choosing that the object chooses itself within us.

It seems comparatively easy to observe my thoughts for only a few seconds, but how can one maintain such a state of observation without making an effort, since it is so easy to identify oneself with one's thoughts?

While you are thinking, you cannot be a witness, since at that moment thought and its object are one. Only afterwards can you know that you have thought. This, you must thoroughly understand. In order to listen to yourself, a certain state of relaxation must settle within you progressively. Hitherto you have tried to reach the mastery of your body by yoga. But when such a technique, such practices are not carried out under the direction of a master who has an authentic tradition behind him, mastering one's body inevitably means bullying it. Whereas to work on one's body should mean that we rid ourselves of it by elimination. After all, the body is nothing but a notion which has been built up and put together by the mind and therefore the mind should be able to free itself of it. The practice of relaxation which you have undertaken is carried out, not only with the idea of freeing yourself from its bondage, but even more so to achieve a transfiguration of the body itself. Our physical body can be glorified if we cease to think about it in our usual way, and when we are able to feel it, not as a resisting and solid mass, but as something subtle and radiant. This result can be obtained by the frequent repetition of an inner attitude. This standpoint of deep relaxation accompanied by a visualization of the body as being more and more fluid and transparent may finally lead us to a real experience of dematerialization. We then understand that the physical opacity of our body is nothing but the consequence of our former and habitual state of fixation and tenseness.

As long as you hold on to the idea of a solid body, whatever the degree of relaxation you may attain, your body nevertheless remains something heavy and stale. But when you become able to recreate your body, when it has become something as light as air, pure and fluid, when its nature is of the very nature of ether, you will see that you have obtained such a result because your attention has been stripped of any strain. At the present moment your attention is all strain and tension. And this state of strain has been strengthened by all the disciplines which you have been subjected to, mainly by concentration.

All disciplines are fixations: discipline excludes everything, except the one thing that one wishes to concentrate upon. Thus one establishes a dictatorship over oneself and all understanding is jeopardized. What is absolutely necessary is attention without strain.

. . . and choiceless.

Choiceless.

. . . and without an end result.

What end result could you possibly arrive at, since the object of your search is unknown? All you can say is this: "When I observe myself, I am really forced to admit that every day I am the prisoner of a thousand unsatisfied desires, or desires whose satisfaction brings me no permanent bliss."

So it seems to me that instead of endlessly running from one desire to another, it would be better to stop and examine the true nature of desire.

If this investigation is successful you will penetrate the nature of the true aim of all desire. What any desire really aims at, is a state of non-desire. This non-desire is a state in which we demand absolutely nothing. Thus it is a state of extreme abundance, of fullness.

This fullness is revealed as being bliss and peace. You now know that you are really seeking nothing else but fullness and absolute peace. Now that you have understood the inner nature of your ultimate goal, you perceive that the ultimate goal is, in fact, not a goal, that is to say an end towards which you strive, but that the ultimate state can only be the consequence of relaxing and letting go. Liberation is not to be obtained by collecting and accumulating, but by being rooted in a state of being which is truly ours and in which we live constantly without knowing it. Even if we wished to, we could not live for a single moment outside of this state.

Might inspiration not be an approach to the path of which you speak? Everyone has problems to solve and everyone has inspirations. Some are helped by spiritual practices, and some by art. In such a state, when one is helped, when one is inspired and things come to meet you, there is a complete letting go of strict attention and reasoning (after lengthy striving of course). In other words, one does not live, but something lives within us. There is a contact with something else. A certain state of duality does subsist, but is not this the kind of approach which could help us towards the path?

I said a few minutes ago that objects have no other significance than to point towards consciousness, but there are of course, certain privileged objects which direct us towards the non-dual experience; works of art are foremost amongst them. When a work of art (whose very nature is to allow itself to be forgotten) causes an inner resonance, the personality disappears, the ego vanishes, and one becomes, for one moment, the very expression of Unity.

I thank you for your answer, but I was thinking of something more definite, that is of artistic creation. At the moment of creation, there is a state. . . I don't like to use this word. . . a mediumistic state, that is to say a state when one is simply a channel between "something else" and that which is going to appear or that which one intends to do. . .

Interrupter. *Yes, one isn't there anymore.*

(Questioner) *Yes one is present! . . . and yet one isn't! . . . There is a giving of oneself, a something which comes to you and urges you to action. Beforehand, of course, one must have worked hard, but at the moment of this gift, this communication between something else which is far away, and that which you are doing, you vanish. The channel is only a channel. May this not be an approach – because after all it is an objective phenomenon, not exactly to be in communication with what one is creating, but with one's self? The approach to knowledge is very difficult – could this not make it easier for some of us? Because, after all, what is knowable is an essence, even if this essence is temporary. If, for instance, we look at a rose, we observe its shape, colour, etc. A quantity of information can be given about the rose, but its very essence nobody knows.*

We know no more than others, we know that it exists, we . . . I mean people who go into things. So perhaps there is in us an essence which may be known in the same way.

Referring to your first remark, you must understand what happens at the moment of the creation of a work of art. By this act, the artist projects himself outwardly. Temporarily the body and mind become perfect instruments of the background and are, as you say, a kind of channel. By means of shape, colour and proportions, they manage to express what is inexpressible.

When you look at a work of architecture whose vertical and horizontal components are in perfect balance, the drive towards the heights and the impression of weight compensate each other to the extent of stripping the building of all its objective mass so that one is carried back, upstream towards the background which is bliss.

Now let us consider your second problem. This we have often analysed. When you think of a rose, you refer to your perception of it and also to your personal way of conceiving it. As you say, you know that such and such a rose has such and such a scent, and its petals are soft to the touch, that it belongs to such and such a botanical species, that it can be made use of in such and such a way; all this is part of the knowledge accumulated by yourself and by men in general, and you superimpose all this on the impression of the rose when you say: "I see a rose". But the real being of the rose, you never see. If you wish to know the rose, it

18

is enough to be yourself. Because our essence and the essence of the rose are the same, since in reality only one essence exists. When you are established in your essence, you communicate with the essence of every separate thing.

Could you speak to us of this inner springing forth which one may observe when truly listening to oneself?

We habitually stop this springing forth by our impatience. What we should do, is be open to it, without striving to handle it, to treat it as the first step of a deductive line of thought, because by doing so we destroy any possibility of real understanding. The quality, the taste, the fullness of this springing forth depend on the purity of our attitude. It may happen that it arises and that it directs us towards something which our ego refuses. In this case we immediately erase it. Sometimes it comes to us later on, and we must show great patience to give it time to ripen.

If we thus get into the habit of observing our daily upsurges, we will become more and more ready to receive the final one. Once we fully realize that non-dual realization cannot be dealt with by the mind because it is beyond the mind, there arises a supreme springing forth which is different from the others. It is simply caused by the elimination of all false identifications, which directs us to the essential part of our being and leaves us in a state which no analysis can reach, because we then no longer exist in a subject-object relationship. It does happen that we know such moments, but our inclination is to by-pass them, since the ego tries to grasp them and turn them into an object of enjoyment, thus warping the experience, transforming it into a caricature. The very desire to prolong this experience causes it to vanish.

Could you speak to us about intuition?

The meaning of the word intuition is direct vision, an immediate grasping of an object known by the subject. Intuition therefore belongs to the realm of duality. *Sadhana* develops intuition, deepening it more and more. All indications given on the attitude of listening are also true of intuition.

When thought comes to an end and one finds oneself in the very midst of oneself, can one and should one remain in such a state?

Are you able to put this question to yourself when you are the state? When you are there, you are there and that is all there is to it.

One thing however is important. That is, to recognize in this experience, that we are open to the Self and not on a mental plane.

Here is something which strikes me as being rather significant, and it happens every day, one does one thing while thinking about another. For instance I often happen to put

my keys down somewhere, and the next moment I can't
remember where they are, because I was thinking of some-
thing else and I was not really present. Is this not a very
ordinary example showing that most of the time we are not
present to ourselves?

Yes it is. We are always somewhere else, living ahead
or behind in time, we long for the future or we regret
the past. We are never really here. This flight in time
is of great significance. If we turn away from the present, or rather if the present is so often unable to hold
our attention, it is because we conceive of it as being a
known and registered reality, therefore devoid of inter-
est, or as a disappointing one. Just so long as we have
not understood that true bliss is not in objects, but in
us, we continue to place our hope in the future and
keep racing ahead. We thus live in a state of imbalance,
bent upon, and striving endlessly towards, the future.

What we must come to understand is that awareness in the present is the only true starting point and
that this starting point is at the same time the point of
arrival.

2

Vedanta is a direct path; its starting point is the deliberate rejection of the subject-object duality which is the framework of all our usual activities (metaphysical speculation included). This path enables us to reach fullness and ultimate bliss without the support of objects. Travelling along this path is an entirely upstream journey implying the complete rejection of all our usual mental activities. Even in their highest form.

He who has understood the entire futility of any search for perfect bliss in the world of duality, can undertake the slow return journey which will bring him back from the exterior to the discovery of his own transcendental reality. The world of names and forms is the result of mental activity. Ignorance *(Avidya)* begins at the very moment when the ego takes names and forms to be separate realities.

It is by the suppression of this ignorance, in other words by attaining knowledge, that all these energies hitherto pointing towards the exterior are brought back, are reversed and leave the world of becoming, thus returning to the unity of being. This reintegration is a spontaneous and necessary result of knowledge. Such a result can only be brought about in the total absence of any effort, by the simple virtue of discernment.

As long as the ego is not intimately and thoroughly convinced of the impossibility of finding happiness in objects, it does not turn towards the non-objective unknown. I repeat "the non-objective unknown", because no quality can be attributed to the Self without it being treated as an object of knowledge.

How can this liberating availability be reached?

I will come back to the necessity of understanding the very nature of desire, because it is important.

Any desire is a search for perfect bliss. This perfect bliss is part of the nature of the Self, therefore all desire is a desire for the Self. Seeking bliss in objects is part of our egotistical make-up. It is because I believe myself to be a distinct being among other distinct beings that I am compelled to search for bliss and the fullness of being by seizing and possessing other beings. Thus we are urged towards a hunt for happiness which is the tragedy of egotistical life. We have taken the first step to freedom when we understand that objects do not contain bliss. The second step is the analysis of the nature of the object, in other words, the recognition that the world of objects, unable as it is to give us bliss, is a purely mental production. This discovery should produce a stilling of the mind, and therefore realization.

The importance and the significance of the stilling of all mental activity must be thoroughly understood; it entails the vanishing of everything which ordinary men call real, that is to say, the world of objects (of which our body and our mind are part). The vanishing of this world of duality and multiplicity alone allows us to discover the reality which is one.

Question
Is consciousness subject to evolution?

Answer
This notion of evolution is one of the most characteristic errors of modern thought.

The error of evolution (or progressivism) is the foremost error of materialism. It is the belief that more can come out of less, that better can be produced by worse. Evolution, in the strict meaning of the word, is only an unfolding, a passing from what is implicit to that which is explicit, from what is not manifested to that which is manifested. It produces nothing. It *never* produces, let alone *creates*. We cannot rely on it in our search for salvation or liberation. Liberation is not a problem of evolution, for no evolution can lead to liberation, which is the result of discernment only.

We are not concerned with evolving, but we should endlessly put the question "Who am I?" to ourselves. By directing our thinking, not towards objects, but towards its own root, one finally discovers the fundamental principle of being. Man possesses, deep within himself, the essence of all wisdom. He may know it or not, but truth is within him and nowhere else.

3

Knowledge without object, which is the theme of these talks, is a non-dual experience; it can be obtained neither by an accumulation of information, nor by any discipline or ascetic practice. In plain language, it is the fact of being aware.

We are completely unaware of our true nature because we constantly identify ourselves with our body, our emotions and our thoughts, thus losing sight of our unchanging centre which is pure consciousness. When we return to our true nature, our thoughts and perceptions no longer appear as modifications of a single substance, they come into being and subside like waves of the ocean.

We have already seen how important it is for us to understand what it is that we are really seeking when we pursue the satisfaction of a desire.

We must therefore begin with the analysis of desire. "What do I want?" Can my desire be gratified by the possession of objects? Objects, are they what I seek? Do they contain what I seek? Let us observe what happens when a desire is satisfied. We see that the gratification of a desire is nothing but its death and that therefore, when we are in search of bliss, we really are pursuing nothing but the death of desire. This proves that our ultimate desire is "non-desire". But "non-desire" appears to our normal consciousness as being blankness. And yet it is in this "blankness" that we must try to probe with open eyes, so as to discover its true nature. In fact, this nothingness is experienced by everybody in infinitesimal gaps which occur between thoughts, each time one desire dies, giving place to the next.

If from time to time we experience moments of stillness and deep attention turned towards these gaps of nothingness, little by little the emptiness will reveal itself as being full, and finally as supreme plenitude. One should adopt this attitude as often and as clearly as possible, thereby allowing it to be more penetrating and effective. With this in view, one should be available, ceaselessly questioning oneself, calmly observing one's own behaviour without passion.

A new and non-objective outlook may then progressively prevail on us and we may come to understand that we are not the ego. We may then, with a complete and new awareness, taste the unexpected flavour of those moments of non-desire which will be revealed as being plenitude, silence, and peace. This flavour which is only fleeting at first will become more constant and vigorous until that time when it will appear as a reality which carries us, enfolds us, and is our very substance. The bliss which is then experienced is entirely different from what we usually call happiness. For at this level of consciousness, one cannot even say "I am happy", since a consciousness which establishes a distinction between a subject and an attribute would be a dual consciousness. We are now speaking of "the Peace of God which passeth all understanding" (St Paul).

We have mentioned watchfulness and availability. It must be understood that these must be perfect in their quality. The quality and the purity of attention which result are the essential conditions of success.

The exercise of this pure attention implies the complete elimination of all elements from the past, thus allowing the authentic purity of the present to be completely grasped. We must forget everything and wait, yet wait for nothing. This entails a state of complete receptivity which seizes and is open to the complete, eternal and perfect newness of each moment.

It is also important that the body should be in a state of perfect relaxation, as the slightest attraction or repulsion results in tensions which impede the purity of attention.

Question
How can I free myself from fear?

Answer
All fear is the inevitable ransom of separateness. As long as we cling to the illusion of being a separate ego, we cannot eliminate fear. The only radical remedy for fear is the realization which restores us to non-dual, global consciousness.

Just as the ego cannot avoid fear, a global unity of consciousness cannot encounter it.

How can one answer the question "Who am I?", as recommended by Ramana Maharshi?

The consciousness of being the "I am" is the basis of consciousness. When we think "I am" and only that, without any qualification, we are pure consciousness without object, the timeless background, the reality which underlies the three states of waking, dreaming and deep sleep. But the moment we say: "I am tired, I am clever, I am a Knight of the Bath. . ." We risk falling into false identifications.

Nothing is jeopardised so long as we say "I am this, I am that" for we understand this to mean the adding of a qualification to the subject. The Fall of Man takes place when consciousness slips into the attribute, thus furthering a loss of the subject as the consciousness of the Self is lost. Such is the fall into multiplicity.

The method of the "Who am I?" advised by the Maharshi is an involutive technique of return to the pure "I am". When I say "Who am I?" and establish my consciousness in a state of empty availability, I make it possible for this consciousness to return to the pure subject. I prevent my consciousness from being attached to any qualification whatsoever, thus putting it in a state of helplessness which enables it to turn back on itself and return to its original purity.

This thought "Who am I?" has a particular virtue

because it is a state of questioning which places the mind face to face with the void. If one has enough honesty and earnestness not to add anything to this void (and on this condition only), the reality of the "I am" must appear.

Does your method of approach imply an active or a passive attitude?

In order to be understood, I am going to give you an example that you already know, because I can find none better.

Certain painters, when they wish to compose the subject of a picture, assemble objects according to their aesthetic sense or their passing fancy, taking one of them as a centre around which they harmonise all the others. Other artists, on the contrary, set aside any idea of a centre. They observe the outline of objects, the way they catch the light, the parts that are shaded, the relationship of space to space, so that no one object is more prominent than any other in the final arrangement, to such an extent that the presence of each object seems to eliminate that of the others. An ensemble is thus obtained, which has neither centre nor outline, and whose presence loses itself in void. It might be said that all authentic works of art have the property of eliminating themselves (as objects), giving place to the Ultimate Reality.

This example shows you that there are two ways of approaching a problem. The first symbolised by the picture with a central object, which one might call "intellectually seizing". In order to grasp a reality, one builds it round a centre by which it may be seized. This method is very useful where the relative world of objects is concerned, but it is entirely ineffective where approach to realization is sought for.

The second method, symbolized by the centre-less picture, can barely be called a method, because it is a methodless method, the "path which may not be named" that Lao-Tze speaks of. If we want to carry it out, we must do as the painter, that is to say, consider all objects and their relationship to each other without striving to find a centre, or to organize them in order to grasp them. It is this letting go of any "grasping" which makes for the efficiency of this method. One has given up any idea of seizing, of taking, of understanding the object, and precisely because of this, the object reveals itself in its infinite truth.

Reality is infinite, thus unseizable. We cannot take hold of it. We can only allow ourselves to be seized.

Is it possible to come to a knowledge of reality by a really deep study of the object?

We said the other day that name and form do not exhaust reality. Name and form do make up the object as an object, but one should not fall into the usual mistake of believing that the object is reality, and that the knowledge of the objects is the knowledge of the whole.

When Linnaeus drew up his botanical classification, he discussed it with Goethe who remarked: "You have all the elements (objects) in your hand, unfortunately, the spirit which is the link between everything is missing." What Goethe calls the "spirit", is the reality which underlies name and form, which our usual scientific knowledge completely disregards.

True knowledge, instead of endeavouring to seize names and forms by defining them as clearly as possible, eliminates and dissolves them. This negative process, apparently nihilistic, leads not to a grasping of reality, but to its revelation as a total unity.

4

Let us return to the subject of "Knowledge without object".

At first this expression might cause a certain uneasiness. How can one know anything which has nothing to do with objectivity? And yet we are constantly established in a non-dual state which we do not perceive. This background is the real link between all things, but through ignorance and mechanical thinking we have taken on the habit of using our intelligence in relation to objects.

If non-objective reality is to be reached, a certain number of obstacles must be eliminated. One must first establish peace in oneself.

Our body, closely knit to our thoughts, is practically always in a state of self-defence or tension, because our thoughts always turn to accumulation and possession. This habit has frozen us into certain moulds, certain clichés which prevent us from delving deeply into ourselves, thus helping us to discern the authentic perspective of reality.

The need to accumulate which is bred into the ego, warps this perspective, leading us to believe that a certain amount of knowledge and certain exercises may help us to reach a state of permanent peace. This belief is ignorance: being at all times established in this peace, there is no need for us to reach it, our true nature is peace. Nothing can be added to it, nothing taken away. The only thing that is required of us is an awareness of the truth of ourselves.

In order to understand the non-dual outlook, we must realize that we are prisoners, slaves to certain "clichés" according to which we always see things in a dual, fragmentary way. If we wish to recover the non-dual outlook, we must get into the habit of reconsidering the "fragmented objects" of our usual knowledge in their relationship one to another, so as to obtain an ever-widening global vision in which the conflicts and oppositions merge into complementary harmony. This global outlook must be widely extended and an ever more harmonious reality will be revealed leading to a vision of oneness.

In the course of this process, one will observe that all problems and conflicts are consequences of a fragmentary outlook. As it becomes less fragmentary, that is more global, we find contradictions becoming oppositions, and oppositions fading so as gradually to become complementary parts. These then appear as aspects of unity. At this point, we have reached the last stage. We stand before an objective unity seized by a subject. There is only one more step before we understand that the subject-object duality is in its turn unreal and that the real is One.

Question
I sometimes experience an inner upsurge which I feel to be very precious, but I never manage to make it take shape and express itself

Answer
One must attentively observe what it is that impedes the outer manifestation. It may be, that at the moment of the upsurge, in your hurry to express it, or maintain it, you obstruct any possible formulation. It may also be that the upsurge is too weak and that its roots are feeble. In that case, you must let if fall of itself, and try to delve into the depths of yourself. This may stimulate a blossoming, giving life to an awareness which previously was not evident. But in no case must you intervene. You must let the upsurge take place, take shape and blossom.

It is nearly always due to a lack of patience, or because we are unable to wait without strain, that the upsurge is impeded. We must remain on the watch a long, long time with no desire to intervene, to grasp nor to make use of it.

5

The "eternal present", our theme in these meetings, lies within the depth of ourselves. It is the eternal awareness of the Self.

Seen from the Ultimate, the world projected by the mind appears and disappears, in other words, it "becomes". When we talk of time and space, it must be thoroughly understood that their reality is relative, it is a reality in the world of becoming. But beyond space-time is that stillness which knows no becoming.

If the background is to be revealed, first of all we must ask the essential question: "Who am I?".

When we say "I", we are identical with the background and this "I" expresses our most intimate self. Each time we say "I think", "I see", "I hear", we qualify it. We associate the "I", the subject, with an object of consciousness, with which we identify ourselves. But if we manage to keep the "I" clear of this identification, then appears the Self, the non-dual, everlasting, unchangeable reality.

I would like the questions put during these talks to be spontaneous, not elaborated. This spontaneity comes if you adopt an attitude of true listening to yourself.

We obviously have to make use of language, but we must try, as we use words, to remain open and to transcend them and feel out the ideas in their true reality, beyond the verbal plane. The hearer may then experience a genuine reaction enabling him to put questions which are truly pertinent.

The path which is here advocated is the direct path. Its process is the elimination of the known, since the experience of the Self, of our true nature, is for the moment unknown to us. The Self can only be described negatively since no positive concept, no part of anything we know, can be applied to it. All thoughts are fragmentations which place us in duality; they set themselves before the Self, thus making unitive knowledge impossible.

It is therefore by discarding the known, that is to say our thoughts, perceptions and emotions, that integration with the ultimate "I", the everlasting present, is possible. The man who experiences this return, who has broken down the limitations set up by the ego, ceases to be tormented by desire and fear. He is in no way diminished by the loss of his individuality, he knows himself to be "out of time". Only such a timeless "I" is entitled to say: "I am".

Whether thoughts appear or not, the eternal Presence remains, transcending the three states (waking, dreaming and deep sleep). Nothing can cause the Sage to return to the level of duality. He is established in an undifferentiated state where the *Atman*, having realised its identity with the *Brahman*, shines of its own light.

Question
All questions put are, in principle, prompted by the ego. It is not the background lying behind the question of course, but the ego (which prompts), hoping thereby to widen its horizon. Nevertheless this questioning ego strives to keep itself at a distance, as far as is possible, so that its questioning may have the widest possible scope. How can this keeping at a distance be made easier?

Answer
When you observe something, you are at the same time this very thing and you are outside it. Let us dwell on this point. You cannot observe the nature of an object if you are not outside it. You cannot taste salt if your mouth is made of salt, you cannot recognise an egotistic state if you are not outside of this state. He who observes must be different from the thing which he observes. But, and this appears to be a paradox, it is also impossible for him to know the nature of an object without being at the same time the very essence of this object. Observing something means therefore that one is at the same time inside and outside it. One is that object. The act of knowing is a challenge to the logical principle of identity, because one might say that knowledge is a unified duality, a dual unity. If this paradox is comprehended, one truly listens, the ego will witness the object, he is all awareness, laying the accent on his non-identity with it. This is in fact a contemplative position which is an authentic attitude. Then true questions may arise if there are any.

In some of the other talks, you spoke of "living knowingly in a state which is not a state". . . Could you help us to understand this?

Strictly speaking it is impossible to talk intelligibly of this state which is not a state. I can only tell you that when this non-dual experience takes place, one knows it. I concede that it is difficult not to be baffled by this concept of non-objective knowledge, that is to say a knowledge where there is no knower of the object. And yet I pray you, even if you are gifted with an active imagination, please make no effort towards this "non-objective knowledge". This knowledge will spontaneously and of itself open your eyes when the time comes.

The important point is that you should eliminate in yourself every element which is not the experience.

Do you think it is possible to go beyond desire and find a state of permanent "well-being"?

Yes, but the transcending of desire can only follow a thorough understanding of its nature. As long as we have not returned to our true being, we are subject to desire. We turn from one object to another, that is to say from one compensation to another. It must be thoroughly understood that if we endeavour to vanquish or transcend desire, this in itself is a desire, and if we strive to be detached while our ego resists with all its might, we are creating a conflict.

True detachment comes when things leave us of themselves. And they leave us as soon as we have really understood that they never keep their promises.

Does the realised man constantly retain this attitude of aloofness when he faces the objective world?

The man who has realised his true nature continues to face all his obligations, to live in society. Simply he is no longer a party to the activities of a society whose only aim is to satisfy the ego. Unbridled accumulation, and ambition, inordinate desire to develop one's individuality, the need to intensify one's personal qualities with an aim in view, all that this implies no longer concerns this man. He is still in the world, but he is not of the world.

If one rejects asceticism, how can one approach realization?

As far as you are concerned, you must begin by drawing up an inventory of yourself. But it is not by drawing up a list of qualities and defects which is more or less accurate that you will make such an inventory, but by observing yourself from moment to moment. Your impulses, those spontaneous reactions which reveal your sympathies and antagonisms, your daily mechanisms, such as judging yourself, will now stand out clearly. You will then notice that your fundamental desire is to try to make all happenings coincide with what you would like to be or to have.

The fact of noticing these things will give birth, albeit tentatively at first, to a habit of standing back from the object. Then, without any action of your will, a certain elimination will take place and, from day to day, you will be less inveigled in what you observe, and one day the independent nature of the beholder will appear to you (there will be nothing left to behold). The beholder will now lose his quality of being a witness and will return knowingly to pure consciousness. When the object and the subject disappear, reality appears. Each thing in its own time. You must first discover those landmarks which point in the right direction. Ascertaining something does not involve creating new bonds, new conditions, it is simply a case of establishing oneself in the state of witness, thus creating a distance between the thing observed and yourself. However, it is very difficult for many people to accept themselves as they are and to bow before the reality of facts. One is always escaping from oneself, one never accepts oneself as one is, because one has fallen into the habit of comparing oneself with a model. At times one sees oneself as superior to this model, at other times, inferior, thus we are always troubled. To reach ultimate knowledge, the only acceptable way is objective vision without choice or judgement.

Why does the ego make its first mistake?

The first mistake does not belong to the ego, it is the mistake which gives birth to the ego and the world at one and the same time. This error is the *"Avidya"* (ignorance) of *Vedanta*, the "Forgetting" of Plato, from which arises fragmentation, that is to say a world with "selves" that believe themselves to be distinct. The ego appears and the world comes into being, its disappearance causes the world to vanish; this is what happens in the state of deep sleep, thus showing us that the world and the ego are one. Beyond the ego and the world stands the everlasting and causeless "I am". That which ignorance has added to this "I am", in other words the ego and the world, knowledge takes away. What then remains is our true nature. But intellectual preoccupations cannot bring about the vanishing of the ego. To us it is only perfect discrimination that reveals the egoless state.

Does man's true nature differ from one individual to another?

When the "I" is stripped of name and form, its unique and indivisible nature remains, and this is the same in all beings. But when false identification deceptively breaks up this "indivisible nature", it gives birth to the illusion that these are separate centres. As long as we identify ourselves with these fragments, that is to say with our body, our impulses, our ideas, no real understanding is possible with others. No system, be it political, philosophical or religious, can alter this.

Beyond the social and revolutionary ideas of a free and brotherly humanity, would there exist the metaphysical

*ideal of a reality where egos, names and forms disappear
and are fused in the one?*

That is so.

*Do you think that a well carried-out psychoanalytical
treatment can lead us to the discovery of our true nature?*

All psychological therapies, psychoanalysis among
them, are based on a point of view which, for *Vedanta*,
is the very cause of what one might call a fundamental
neurosis, a metaphysical neurosis, which is the arising
of an ego believing itself to be separate.

The aim of psychoanalysis is to restore health and
balance to this separate ego which it considers as a
justified reality. The psychoanalyser wishes to restore
a balanced and harmonious ego, an ego in harmony
with its surroundings and with other creatures. This
ideal appears on second thoughts to be entirely naive.
When we wish to be a balanced self we, in fact, wish
to prolong an imbalance under the best possible conditions by appealing to energies which may reinforce,
fix and establish an egotistic state which is really the
basic imbalance, the source of all others. This is just as
absurd as fighting the symptoms of an illness without
applying oneself to the illness itself. The psychoanalytical cure is therefore not really a cure. It does not rid
the sick man of his sickness, it helps him to live it, with
the ego. His sickness is an imaginary one. From the
Vedanta point of view, a psychoanalyst works always,

be it unconsciously and in all honesty, like "Monsieur Purgon", the doctor in Molière's "Malade Imaginaire". A true Master knows that what we usually call health and balance is in fact imbalance and sickness. He will not endeavour to steady an imbalance, to uphold by props what is about to fall; he will strike at the fundamental imbalance, the original error, thereby establishing that true health which can only exist as a result of our feeling of unity with the whole.

What can we do to eliminate the social and economic fetters and impediments? Are certain professions not in opposition to spiritual research? Just imagine the conditions of a man who works in an armament factory! He knows very well that the thing that he makes will sooner or later spread pain and death. What can he do?

This question concerns a particularly difficult problem: the relationship between social life and spiritual research.

The "traditional societies" (in Guénon's meaning of the word) were constructed so as to allow man to live on earth and gain heaven in the best possible way. Conflicts obviously did arise between the temporal and spiritual needs, but there was never a fundamental opposition because no one dared to doubt the primacy of God over Caesar. Nowadays, Caesar negates God, or even claims to assume his place. In communist countries the supreme values are social; in capitalist countries, they are power and money. What is spiritual is denied, belittled or ignored. Modern man is therefore at a terrible disadvantage where spiritual research is concerned.

However, this disadvantage must not be exaggerated. As the desire for the spiritual increases, all social life becomes less binding, and a much simpler adaptation is sooner or later established. As soon as a man really awakens to spiritual life, certain incompatible conditions become unbearable, inacceptable, and he then lets go of certain things, he changes his profession, he re-adapts himself; such a re-adaptation must be neither forced nor willed and, above all, not anticipated. It happens naturally and spontaneously as the spiritual orientation asserts itself clearly.

A religious man whose faith is deep and authentic, and who completely trusts God, with full and entire love, such a man may he not come upon this impersonal and unified life of which we speak?

We cannot clearly understand the question without probing into the meaning of the word "Love".

In his "Banquet", Plato defines love as being the desire to possess permanently what is good. But the desire or the love of good is only conceivable if there is a knowledge, a previous experience or a memory of the good. One might thus say that any love is a home-sickness, a longing for a lost paradise.

The man who lives in a condition where he knows no liberating activity, lives in a world of pain and sadness which from time to time gives place to sparks of joy. All human endeavour strives towards the keeping and the prolonging of such moments.

The mistake that most men make is to believe that these moments of joy are caused by the conditions which precede them.

It is a long and arduous task to free oneself from this error. What may help us is when we notice how relative are such joys which, as we very soon see, are not always produced by the same conditions, since what is a condition of joy for one man is not so for another, and what was the condition of yesterday's joy is no more so today. Thus a man finds himself on the threshold of true spiritual research which begins with a return to oneself. This is the first step towards the Self.

In treading this path, one gradually discovers joy without object, unconditional joy, the very joy of our being. In the beginning therefore we find love, which is desire for perfect joy. This love, as we have seen, implies a knowledge or a memory of joy. In itself it is only a pure driving energy. The outcome of the search depends entirely on the way in which energy is employed. We all love bliss and we love bliss only. As is said in the *Brihadaranyaka Upanishad*, "we do not love creatures for themselves, but only for the bliss of the Self which they contain".

Love will be enlightened when we come into contact with that bliss which is free from any condition or object. It must be thoroughly understood that we have no need to acquire love, because in the depths of ourselves we are "desire for perfect bliss", or in theological language: "love of God". No one needs to acquire nor to increase love, but only to enlighten it on its true aim.

This saving knowledge is obtained by the elimination of fragmentary knowledge, by the awareness that objects can neither contain nor produce bliss. And this awareness is finally an act of discrimination. A chance is offered to us for this discrimination to emerge at every moment of joy. Each moment of joy allows us to see the essential difference between its "foundings" and joy. Every time this discrimination is experienced in full consciousness, there is access to pure joy, discovery of being and identification of one's being with total being.

The love and abandon of the authentic *bhakti* is the result of a purification of love by knowledge. Otherwise it is only a sentimental urge, quite valueless for liberation.

It is important not to mistake the letting go of that passion which results from merging with the object, with the letting go of liberating love which is an illumination due to knowledge.

This is the fundamental distinction between idolatry and religion. The surrender to an object, the merging with an object, are comparatively easy. Nothing is easier than to discover a somewhat beautiful, good and powerful thing and to have a marvellous sense of exaltation by giving oneself over to it. Idolaters taste deep joy as long as they do not overstep the limitations of their idol, as long as the idol does not crumble of itself. Napoleon's soldiers, the Grognards, knew perfect joy until the day of Waterloo. The only drawback to idolatry is the disproportion between the finite and the infinite. Man's desire for happiness is infinite and that is why no object – that is to say, no finite reality – can fill it. All idolatry is therefore either illusion or failure.

I have often heard it said that without the help of Yoga, metaphysical realization can be very difficult. What do you think about it?

To begin with Yoga is a harmonization of the body, to prevent it from being an impediment to spiritual research. It is also a set of techniques tending to the ending of all mental activity. It is a method of voluntary effort and systematic purification, leading to a state of mental stillness *(Samadhi)*.

Samadhi can be experienced as bliss or emptiness. In the case of bliss, it remains in the world of duality. In the case of emptiness, it is the last stage in duality, but it does not throw it off. The emptiness of *Samadhi* takes place when the object has reached its ultimate simplification. One might say that it is pure object, without any qualification whatsoever, an object which is object and nothing else. This is why it is a barrier, the last barrier, to realization. Sooner or later, *Samadhi* experienced as emptiness, will reveal its duality and the longing for unity will appear.

This meeting with emptiness is something absolutely new; and it may easily be mistaken for realization. Then there occurs a tendency to settle in this emptiness which one has learnt to produce. It is comforting to pacify the ego and to taste this emptiness. But one should not mistake the taste of a silent mind with the experience of which I am speaking. This taste is still an object, it has to be abandoned, the last step has to be taken, for the Yogi who does not awaken to the Experience, is in a situation which, from a certain point of view, may be considered worse than that of the ordinary man. Indeed, when he returns from the state of *Samadhi* to find those usual objects which had been temporarily eliminated by a voluntary technique, he runs the risk of rediscovering them with an increased virulence.

Samadhi experienced as joy is in fact a state in which one enters and from which one emerges. Sooner or later its insufficiency is felt. The man who leaves this joy, falls back in to the world of objects. He has no precise memory of his experience which, since it belongs to a supra-mental reality, can leave no mental trace (memory), but nevertheless he remains in a state of shock, of exaltation, of longing which is a source of confusion. Such is the result of the Yogic path.

In the direct path we, by discrimination, come to the conviction that ultimate reality lies beyond any physical or mental framework. As a sideline, we make use of Yoga to loosen certain knots, or do away with certain disturbances. But we never lose sight of the non-dual background. Liberation is not reached by subservience to certain more or less strict rules, but by knowledge

which wipes out time, space, cause-and-effect. A return
to ignorance is now excluded.

6

The everlasting present is completely unrelated to time and space. Therefore it has no link with the past, the future or any given place. In its very essence, it is reality, *"hic et nunc"* (here and now). Since this reality lies outside any mental framework, it cannot be expressed, communicated or known by any means but by pure experience alone. From this background, thought, and with it the world of multiplicity, arises and then back to it returns. When the mind is in any way active, this background is consciousness as witness, absolutely non-involved. When mental activity ceases, it is pure objectless consciousness. This background is our true nature and can only be revealed spontaneously, i.e., in an attitude devoid of any striving, of any premeditation, any intention. This reality, being formless, escapes any qualification whatsoever. However, the traditional words peace and bliss are nearest to expressing it.

This background can be perceived in each interval that occurs between two thoughts or two perceptions. In such intervals one may come upon the timeless moment, in other words, the eternal present. But this is hindered by our belief that what has no form is unreal. Whenever we encounter this perception of the formless we mistake it for a blank or absence which in its turn creates a feeling of uneasiness. This discomfort (the fear of the void) urges us to search for another thought or perception which will fill the dreaded void.

This void terrifies us because it denies being. As long as we are unable to conceive being in any aspect other than form, the presence of the formless (the background) gives us a false impression of emptiness which we immediately strive to fill with forms (objects).

In this way we by-pass a marvellous chance of being. Let us observe for example the way a nervous or anxious man breathes. Such a man does not venture to breathe out fully, he does not dare to empty his lungs and remain at peace until the moment when the in-breathing phase comes of itself. This is a symptom of deep fear and anxiety. When the lungs are empty an anxious man is in dread of the void, and he gives himself over to the movement of breathing in so as to recover his habitual feeling of life and a state of passing relief.

But in the case of a healthy man, that is a man who is perfectly harmonised, in agreement with himself and the cosmos, breathing has a metaphysical significance, it is the symbol of the rhythm of exchange between the individual and his principle. Each breathing out expresses an entire surrendering of the creature to God and each inspiration signifies the return of the divine influx.

Between the two moments, at the moment when the lungs are empty, the unmanifested divine is approached.

Thus we can see how fear hinders us from being and experiencing the formless.

7

As did the philosophers in Classical times, so do the Sages of traditional India continue to use today the dialogue form to impart true knowledge.

If it is to bear its fruit, such a dialogue requires a particular type of listening. That is, an effortless attention devoid of any strain, which reveals the deepest recess of the listener's being. It is indeed most important to listen not only to the teacher but also to everything which surges up from the depths of one's inner self. Through such an attitude we are spontaneously led, without conflict, to a state where we are receptive to essential knowledge. Then arise those true questions which are the props and the starting points of the search. This search proceeds by the reduction and the elimination of questions. These become more and more inadequate until the moment when the disciple sees that perfect understanding can only be reached by the absence of questions, by silence. This silence has in itself a taste of peace and bliss. It is not emptiness, it is not ignorance, it is fullness and complete knowledge.

Any knowledge, except knowledge of the Self, is knowledge of an object. Thus the Self can only be known non-dually. Following such knowledge, the Self is revealed as pure objectless consciousness of pure bliss.

We live in a world of objects which are forever changing. Even our mind is in a state of perpetual change. We have an impression of universal becoming. This is because we have completely forgotten that the Self (the supreme subject) underlies the ego and the world of which it is an unmoving motive power and the ultimate knower. *Sadhana* is nothing else but a return to the consciousness of the unmovable and blissful Self which is the root of ourselves and all objects. This losing sight of the consciousness of the Self is described in the *Vedantic* tradition as a process of identification with objects. It is a kind of forgetfulness, of fascination, of attraction. The myth of Narcissus is a perfect llustration of this fall into the object, the seeming absorption of the Self into the wave of *Samsara*. From this moment onwards, the Self has forgotten itself, paradise is lost and an ego arises, an ego which says: "I do this, I suffer, I think". By virtue of this identification, what is impersonal becomes mistakenly personal. The search for happiness becomes a desperate search, for the ego – having lost its consciousness of the Self, of perfect bliss – now seeks happiness in finite and passing objects. Sooner or later however, the ego will be impelled to see the impossibility of finding true happiness in objects and in separate beings, thus verifying Schopenhauer's statement according to which "Life is a battle undertaken in the certainty of being beaten".

If one is to extricate oneself from this predicament, one must distinguish the real from the unreal. In all our daily activities, we have the feeling of being an active agent. This feeling is both true and illusory. I can say that I am truly an agent in all my actions, in so far as I am the supreme subject, the Self. I begin to go wrong from the moment when I grasp myself as being an active subject. Since the only true active subject is the immovable Self, it cannot be apprehended by the mind.

It can be known solely as a non-objective principle beyond the mind. This is why all our efforts to apprehend the subject intellectually, necessarily lead to the illusion of a mind-body ego, author of these actions. Nevertheless this mind-body is not a real agent: it is only an instrument of the manifesting Self, the only true subject, the only true agent. The ego's mistake arises at the moment when I forget that any activity of the mind-body is that of an instrument. This error is the confusion between instrument and agent. It is in some way the agent which loses itself in the instrument.

Liberation is reached when I understand that the me seen as a mind-body is not the subject-agent, but the real subject-agent is the I, the Self, the pure subject.

By going over this theme as often as possible, I gradually loosen the me, the mind-body, a mere instrument. This loosening allows the Self to awaken to its own substance.

Question
As you have just said, the error that lies at the root of our

61

human tragedy which places bliss in the object, is so strong that we do not know how to attain this discrimination, this objectless joy which you describe in your study "From Desire to Joy without an Object". How can we go beyond this conditioning?

Answer
First of all, it is important to realize that what we are really after is a perfectly stable state which at the same time would be joy, peace and supreme security. Unfortunately, life gives us no promise of stability and the joy given by a desired object is always a fleeting one.

What is the exact relationship between a fleeting joy and the objects which give it? At first sight, it seems to be a relationship of cause and effect, or of container and contained, but experience shows us that the same object can at different moments produce joy, disgust or complete indifference. This goes to prove that it does not produce joy, it merely triggers it off.

When the coveted object is finally possessed, we find ourselves in a state of non-desire and joy is nothing else but the attainment of such a state. When joy is perfect and non-desire is complete, the object vanishes. Only joy remains. For the ego it is a stopping point.

Thus the object is in no way necessary for this arrest in desire. Wisdom (i.e. the science of happiness) is nothing else but the know-how of "stopping". Thus an objectless stilling of desire is achieved, and thereby arises perfect joy.

This perfect joy which we sought in objects is revealed

as being the basis of being. The understanding of this truth may be considered as the basis of realization.

Is the way you indicate not too arid, too bleak? Do you not think that emotion which in certain doctrines is considered as an agent of discovery may be of great help?

As long as man is an ego, he faces every situation from the point of view "I like"–"I don't like". Due to this, he is plunged into emotionalism and the ability to see things as they are is impossible for him. Discrimination, which is the only decisive factor in knowledge, is completely impervious to emotionalism. In no case can emotion further an approach to authentic knowledge.

Emotion is *Rajas*. According to the Hindu doctrine, the last phase before liberation is *Sattva*. *Sattva* is serenity, truth and light. A sattvic atmosphere is the necessary condition of any authentic discrimination. He who is impersonal, egoless, has decisively left the emotional plane behind. Such is the state of perfect freedom. He no longer approaches things from the point of view "Pleasant-unpleasant"; he deals with situations without the intervention of any personal choice. He therefore lives the present situation as it occurs, with perfect simplicity and adequacy. Thus he never comes up against what the ordinary man calls suffering. This change of axis from an emotional attitude to an impersonal one is never the result of an effort. It is the consequence of discrimination alone which allows us to grasp the difference.

Are there stages in this realization?

There are stages in elimination, but none in realization. Realization is nothing other than that reality which lies beyond becoming and which for this reason is completely outside the framework of time, space, cause and effect.

If one is to go beyond time, space and cause, it is impossible to make use of time, space and cause. Therefore, in true realization there is no stage, no motivation.

Realization is of its own nature, instantaneous, abrupt, everlasting. If a cause is used as a prop, one will be led to another cause. Having covered a distance, one finds oneself before another one and the same is true of Time. No process of becoming can help us to quit becoming. What is everlasting does not ripen in Time.

In the course of this search, does the Self make itself felt by a force which is usually called Grace?

When the impersonal outlook has been revealed to you, the Self is like a magnet and a light which attracts and guides. Everything which issues from the Self is pure Grace, that is, it is neither a result, nor a compensation and above all, not a reward. Nevertheless this Grace should not be conceived of in the Jewish-Christian spirit as an arbitrary choice. The Self does not choose. It shines like the sun for any eyes that are open and turned towards it.

May one speak of an appeal from the Self?

Yes, but such an appeal must be understood in a very special sense. It may be said that the Self is an appeal in so far as it is a presence, and it is up to us to be aware of its radiance. Our answer to this appeal places us in a perspective where everything is turned upside down.

If all is turned upside down has not life lost all its flavour? How is one to find the strength to accept life?

This change is something of a paradox. In one sense, one might say that things have lost their flavour, but at the same time they have recovered their true flavour hitherto unsuspected. Such words as "to accept" or "to bear" life no longer have any meaning, because the old categories of good and evil, pleasant and unpleasant, have completely vanished, giving place to an unique flavour, the flavour of the Divine, the revelation of that *Ananda* which was hitherto hidden by the *nama-rupa* (names, forms and separate objects).

Thus the meaning of the dying words of Bernanos' Curé de Campagne "Everything is Grace", springs to life.

I sometimes go through moments when I feel completely engulfed in an accumulation of contradictory thoughts, their mass overwhelms me and I get the impression of being unable to reach a state of peace. I am overwhelmed to such an extent that I feel carried away by a flood and I cannot extricate myself. Of course, time passes, days go by, I am once more steady and a state of detachment is re-established. But there are unbearable moments. What can be done during such moments?

Your complaint is one of the characteristic curses of our modern world. Modern man is a creature whose digestive tract and mind are practically always overcrowded. (There is a strong link between these two types of overcrowding.) The first thing to do is to relieve the mind and abstain from treating it like a garbage can into which are poured all the residues of radio, television, the daily press and detective novels.

The second is not to treat one's stomach as a receptacle which is undiscerningly crammed with all the products of the modern food industry. This having been achieved, the work is quite straightforward.

This work is mainly an effort to grasp the nature of thought. It must be understood that the action of thinking is an action of desiring, and the stopping of thought coincides with a stopping of desire. Mental therapy is therefore a therapy of desire.

We have reached the fundamental problem: What is desire? What is the ultimate object of desire? How can desire be quenched?

Let us state briefly that desire could be described as the thirst for perfect bliss. This perfect bliss *(Ananda)* is the inner essence of the Self. Therefore all desire is a desire for the Self. But we imagine that we desire objects. If we wish to quench desire, or to satisfy it – which amounts to the same thing – we must realise that we do not desire objects, but the Self; and that the Self is not far away from us, outside us, but that it is "ourselves". What quenches desire is therefore the discovery of the Self, which comes about when one has understood that it is not *the object* which is desired.

I would like to come back to the question of emotion. I think a man must have suffered, must have loved, must have gone through a certain number of disappointments before he reaches discrimination. It seems to me that emotion must precede discrimination, for the man who has neither loved nor suffered deeply cannot, so it seems to me, know discrimination, because he feels no need to examine himself.

In the mind of western man, there is nearly always a tendency to overrate suffering. This tendency is inherited from Christianity and Romanticism. One has, for centuries, considered suffering to be an atonement, a purification, and a cause of uplift. Suffering may comprise such virtues but not necessarily so. What exactly is the true value of suffering? It is that of a symptom. Suffering is the sign of a mistake, a wrongly directed desire. It is not in itself an error, it is a consequence, the symptom of a mistake and, being a symptom, it is of value in so far as it is understood as such. Suffering in itself is absolutely useless. What is useful, is to understand what particular mistake it is a symptom of. In this sense, and in this sense only, one can say with Musset: "L'homme est un apprenti. La douleur est son maître". Man is an apprentice and suffering is his master, but that does not mean that suffering is the only teacher.

All events are our teachers so long as we fully understand what they signify. To reach discrimination, suffering is not necessarily more useful than joy. One as well as the other may be a guide, in so far as we are capable of understanding them.

What does it mean to understand the joys and pains of life?

It is understanding how false they are. Let us recall Kipling's sentence: "If you can meet with triumph and disaster and treat those two imposters just the same." What is meant by the "two imposters"? Triumph is what fortifies the ego, and disaster is what destroys it. Now the ego is an error. The error of separatism, of the wave which takes itself to be distinct from the ocean. Triumph is therefore necessarily a liar, it is but a lull, and sooner or later the wave will return to the ocean. In the same way disaster is a liar, for the tumbling of the wave is the end of nothing. A wave which loses itself in the ocean does not lose a drop of its water. It only loses its name and its form, that is its limits; in fact all that is negative about it. Its positive reality (water) cannot perish. Therefore what is important is neither pleasure nor pain, success nor failure, what is important is to understand that neither of them have any importance whatsoever. This understanding calls for peace, calm and serenity.

Are there moments in the day which are more favourable than others for these exercises of attention to oneself or may they be practised at any moment?

The most favourable moments are the early morning, two hours before sunrise (matins) and early evening at the time when the sun sets (complines). The early morning is pre-eminently favourable because this is the time when nature is in a state of deepest rest. Sunset is not as beneficial, but it favours the return to oneself, because both man and nature are in a phase of relaxation. When such relaxation is not impaired by a state of fatigue, it is conducive to meditation and inner contemplation. We should not forget that any moment in the day when we feel empty, unoccupied, available, be it only for a few seconds (it is not a question of time, it is a question of quality) is an occasion. In religious terms I might say that they are a call to contemplation.

What do you think of those techniques of meditation which are so fashionable at present?

Any technique is a conditioning, and those techniques of meditation which claim to uncondition, remain within a vicious circle. To meditate is to do something, and this cannot be denied under the pretext that this doing aims at cessation and at doing nothing.

The man who meditates methodically is like a man who is getting ready to go on a journey. If you do not

69

intend going on a journey, there is nothing to be done about it, you just don't start. If you wish to be available and open to the light of the Self, there is nothing to do about that. There is no necessity to do something in order to do nothing. There is just nothing to be done. True meditation is a sequence of moments of grace, peace and letting-go.

Nevertheless certain techniques of meditation may be useful if we thoroughly understand that they have no more than an educational value. The ordinary man is so busy, so restless, that it is quite a business for him to learn how to approach a state of doing nothing. Such techniques are no more than techniques of approach. With their help we do not achieve the state of doing nothing, but they allow us to draw near it. Realization is impossible if we do not go beyond them.

Generally speaking, these techniques come under two headings which may be named meditation with an object, and meditation without an object.

Meditation with an object is the easier of the two and is best suited for beginners. An object of contemplation, concrete or abstract, is agreed upon: Krishna, Jesus, Divine Goodness, the Magnificence of God. The meditator concentrates on this image or concept. He visualizes the image or defines the concept in its general outline and in its details. It may happen that at the end, his meditation merges him with the object, thus he knows a state of unity. This is but a state however, it is not realization. Nevertheless, being pre-eminently still and peaceful, the meditator may by chance accede to realization in which he falls from a qualified state of unity into a Oneness.

This fall is not a necessary consequence of such a state (since in no case can it be the consequence of anything), but it may be said that this state of unification between the meditator and his object, is a state which favours unconditioning.

Meditation without an object is an abrupt and direct path suited to those who have a considerable power of abstraction and discrimination. This technique always requires the presence of a qualified master. It implies elimination, reduction and involution: it is an exercise in comprehension of the ultimate nature of the object, leading the meditator to realize that the reality of the object is the subject.

One first observes that the object has no reality except its relationship to the subject, that an object without a subject is unthinkable. Yet one should be careful not to treat the subject and the object as equivalent and corresponding poles, because reality is not transcendent but transcendental.

It is a process of eliminating objects.

It should be well understood that the word "object" signifies not only objects of the physical world and our body, but also any psychic reality, i.e. emotions, images, thoughts. By practising the negation of objects, of more and more of them and more and more radically, leading to the total elimination of objective reality, one comes to discover that, beyond the vanishing of the object (which has in consequence led to the vanishing of the

71

subject) there remains the Self, a pure and objectless consciousness, pure objectless love, and infinite bliss.

This procedure is the intellectual aspect of meditation without object. If it is to be truly effective it should be completed by its emotional component.

In this case the object is contemplated as a desired goal. Deeper thinking shows us that desire towards an object is in fact desire, not so much of the object, but for something which the object appears to contain or to produce, that is bliss, peace, joy which is fullness and completeness. Thus one realizes that desire is not in fact directed towards the object but towards the reality underlying the object. At this point one has covered considerable ground, because one now knows that we do not in fact desire things. The reality of the object is now completely bereft of its value and desire is at a loss for a goal.

The outer world loses its attraction and desire falls back upon itself.

Thus one reaches realization of the Self. No exact definition of this realization can be given, since it lies beyond duality and cannot be grasped by language. One can, however, endeavour to describe it by saying that the realized man is one who has reached a pure and full consciousness of "I am". For the ordinary man, such a consciousness is always confused because it is impure, that is to say, accompanied by qualifications. "I am this or that", "I have to deal with this or that". In reality this "I am" is ever there, it can't be otherwise. It accompanies each and every state. To return to the "I am" in its complete purity, there is no other way than the total elimination of everything that accompanies it: objects, states. Then that consciousness which hitherto used to turn to the innumerable companions of the "I am", sees them all to be lifeless, finds itself, and realizes its own everlasting splendour.

This path seems extremely rapid, if one can of course apply it.

We cannot describe it as quick or slow, all we can say is that it is the most direct. Direct paths are not necessarily the quickest because they are the most difficult. The main obstacle to this meditation without object is that it demands of us a type of understanding to which we are not accustomed. Our desire for harmony and fulfilment constantly urges us to change ourselves. Whereas the mind can never change anything. When I say "change" I mean to leave the idea of change behind. When you have turned towards this objectlessness, these problems vanish because you know that they are purely self-created.

Are ascetic practices not necessary to clean the house, don't we need a discipline to keep it clean?

One can never clean the house with those very factors which have created what you call "dirt". The mind can never be altered by the mind.

8

True knowledge, that is to say, absolute knowledge, differs from relative knowledge by the complete vanishing of the subject-object duality. Only when the object ceases to be an object, as a result of the upsurging of the One, does one experience this knowledge. The elimination of all that is objective leads us to a silence which is neither a nothingness, nor an impression of absence, but is immediate (non-mediate) knowledge of oneself. The flavour of this silence is experienced as non-objective presence, peace, joy and bliss.

From habit we have created a pattern by which we see ourselves as actor and thinker, and we are thus led to endless conflicts and pain. I should like to dwell on this identification with the thinker or the actor.

At the very moment when we act, consciousness is one with the action. Nothing exists for us outside the action. At the very moment when we think, consciousness is nothing but thought and there is no duality. It is only after the action or the thought, that there arises the process of dual thinking and identification. This, the subject-object relationship, replaces the original unity of the conscious action. But since the true subject, the Self, lies beyond the consciousness of name and form, the quality of subject and agent will be associated with this element of form, that is the mind, the psychic reality which conditions action. It is this psychic reality which will be set up as the ego, as a "me", that is to say an active, separate and formal reality. Then, we say: "I did that. I thought that, I endured that". Whereas in fact the true subject, the Self, transcends all becoming and any formal reality. The supreme knower remains completely distinct from anything we know. Thus, in this sense it is unknowable. Unknowable, here, means that it cannot be grasped as an object. This is why the upsurge of the ultimate subject can only take place after the universe of forms and objects has completely vanished.

The supreme knower is ever present during change, and when change ceases, it is pure presence. It is only the ego which obscures this presence. This primordial notion of the total, immovable, infinite presence, the presence of the Self to the Self, must be a constant object of meditation – it being well understood that meditation, in our meaning of the word, is not a meditation carried out at a given time, but a constant and acute awareness of this presence throughout our daily life.

This meditation should not be considered as accumulation, but on the contrary as elimination, which does not lead to a letting-go but to a spontaneous losing of the becoming process. It is like a journey which begins with sensational events, the primeval forest, the jungle, the steppes, and finishes with a desert at the end of which we may witness an indescribable sunrise.

Meditation should be visualized. By the word "visualized" I mean that one's attention should be fixed on all images, be it a matter of seeing, hearing or touching, etc. One should go step by step without hurry. Here more than anywhere, one must not be impatient. Nothing is urgent, we are not aiming at a conclusion. We must thoroughly understand that things that are known cannot help us to reach an unknown end. The unknown always reveals itself spontaneously and independently of ourselves. We should therefore avoid any wish to seize, to grasp or to force anything.

All we can do is expect without expectation. I repeat without expectation, because expectation is always directed towards an object, thereby causing a projection which hinders the revelation of the unknown. The only thing we can do is be constantly aware of this process, which brings us back from the object to the supreme subject. Thus your vision of yourself will have changed. Then, instead of trying to modify each situation in the hope of bringing about a more favourable outcome, you realize the uselessness of intervening.

When some half-filled glasses of water stand on a sloping tray, one may try to stand them level by using props. But it is much easier to simply straighten the tray. Otherwise it will be a long, complicated and uncertain business only to arrive at a precarious state of balance. Our mistake is that we want to straighten the objects one by one, which is an unending process, instead of straightening the tray, i.e., the basis. As soon as that is put right, everything falls into its right place.

Question

Don't you think it is a good thing to hear the same things over and over again, in spite of the drawbacks of repetition, because one may thus grasp them more thoroughly?

Answer

I quite agree. It is also important, if you observe a reaction and see that it entails a certain insufficiency, to be able to express it. Once put clearly into words, you sometimes find that it is no longer necessary to put the question. A question which is well thought out and put into words sometimes yields its own answer. When you are alone with yourself, do not question with impatience, do not fabricate questions in order to get answers in accordance with your outlook. Allow the answer to arise of itself.

When one speaks of realization one thinks of a state of unity. It seems to me that there are several ways of being in a state of unity. In our everyday life, when one is absorbed in his work, or in an object, one is immersed and lost in it. When Archimedes was working on geometry, it could be said that Archimedes was geometry. On the other hand, if one embarks upon the practice of meditation on the theme of the discrimination between the seer and the seen, one experiences a different unity, unity of the pure subject, stripped of any object. Could you define the relationship between these two forms of unity?

The apparent duality of the seer and the seen, or the

subject and the object, is a sort of crutch. When one has applied this method for a certain time, the seer ceases to be the seer because the seen has become a simple prolongation of his being. There is therefore strictly speaking no more seen since the seen is recognized as the very nature of the seer.

At the beginning, we are more or less absorbed in what we do, we are lost in the object. In order to free ourselves from the object and reach the unitive knowledge of the subject, the method of discrimination between the seer and the seen may be considered as a sort of crutch. This gradually leads us to the understanding that we are neither perception nor thought, but He who knows. Then we arrive at a non-involvement. The climax of this non-involvement is an experience of the unity in the subject, but the unity which is thus reached is not ultimate.

Of these two experiences of unity we have described, that of absorption in the object and that of absorption in the subject, neither is supreme, since the first leads to the vanishing of the subject and the second to the vanishing of the object. Contrary to the other two, the unity which is that of realization does not eliminate, it totalizes and unifies. It is a consciousness of the unity of the subject-object. These three experiences of unity are the three stages which the Zen masters refer to: "Before you enter into the study of the Path, mountains are mountains and rivers are rivers; in due course mountains are no longer mountains, nor are the rivers, rivers; but when Illumination shines forth, mountains are mountains again and rivers are rivers."

Does the discernment you have reached allow you to stand aloof from injustice or any other kind of pain and not be affected by them? Does this not prevent you from taking part in active charity, but allow you to isolate yourself in an ivory tower?

What is called evil or injustice is fundamentally nothing more than an error, or more exactly an ignorance. One is blind to the fact that all things are fundamentally one. Every event, rightly viewed, that is to say seen in its true relationship with the totality, is right and just. In a global and authentic perspective, in a true one, evil and injustice do not exist. This point is most important. As long as it has not been accepted, no true understanding is possible. One stands above and aloof from evil, exactly in so far as one develops a capacity for global vision. Global, that is to say non-egotistic, non-selfish, non-partial, non-fragmentary.

However, it is important not to mistake this aloofness with regard to evil which is a transcending and a liberation, with selfishness and common indifference. The detached man's behaviour may somewhat resemble that of someone who is basely indifferent, whereas true detachment has no point in common with indifference. The detached man is detached from himself and from objects. In consequence, he knows no reaction of fear, hatred or desire. The sufferings and troubles of others do not affect him any more than his own, and he sees himself to be in unity with all beings. He constantly widens and transforms fragmentary points of view into global ones.

The usual methods used against evil, which consist in neutralizing an urge with its opposite, are repugnant to and do not concern the detached ma; he sees their vanity, their uselessness. In consequence he sometimes appears to be selfish and indifferent. He is in fact, despite appearances, the only active man; but a global vision cannot be forced or handed out like a piece of cake, it can only be communicated to a man who is ripe for it.

What is likely to lead someone who has never heard about it to this discernment or this aloofness of which you speak? Indeed this path appears most extraordinary and many people spend the whole of their lives without ever hearing of it and without perceiving any hint of such a search.

The first thing that should be understood is that the ordinary man, he who neither knows nor has any idea of this path, is in a situation which is entirely false. The egotistic outlook being an entirely mistaken one, those men who have not lost the illusion of their separateness, live and die in error. The specific character of error and illusion is that, sooner or later, they come up against opposition and contradiction. These oppositions and contradictions are the landmarks which urge us towards the path. Each pain, each failure urges us to think, to turn our observation on ourselves and to see that the fundamental error of our lives is the build-up of an ego which believes itself to be distinct and separate. It is therefore neither by chance nor by accident that we are led to spiritual research.

We may be awakened to this research by each and every event of our life in the exact measure in which we are capable of understanding them and of grasping their inner truth.

Seen from this point of view, one can well understand the Stoics, according to whom events are in themselves indifferent, neither good nor evil. What is good or evil is the use we put them to according to the depth of our understanding. Our search therefore is never the result of blind chance. It is that of our capacity for truth. That is why it is often said in the East that the man who is ripe for his guru finds him, and the man who does not find him is not a victim of bad luck or of fate, but only of his lack of maturity.

All spiritual masters condemn violence. But up to what point is it possible to be non-violent? Are there not cases when the spiritual man himself can resort to violent behaviour?

All acts of violence are in principle born from egotistical states. An egoless man is therefore, in principle, non-violent. But non-violence should not be turned into a sort of taboo. There are certain definite cases where the use of force, of compulsion, even violence, is imperative. In such cases the egoless man will make use of such force and may apparently act with violence. But it goes without saying that this will be a mere appearance since his action is completely devoid of desire or fear. This outlook allowed Krishna to urge Arjuna to fight and do his duty as a *Kshatriya*.

It should be thoroughly understood that authentic non-violence has nothing in common with cowardice or passivity. But in the same way that a man who is compelled to suffer from force is not necessarily non-violent, it is not because one employs force that one can rightly be called violent. The right question is this: "Is non-violent employment of force conceivable?" I answer "Yes". But qualify this by saying that it is very unusual, in fact exceptional.

The non-egotistic man, from his very nature, neutralizes violence and spreads around himself the peace which is within him. However, he may be led – I repeat very exceptionally – to employ force, his motivation being pure, that is non-egotistic. The man who has been through the experience sees that his neighbour is wrong because his vision of being is fragmented. At the same time, he sees in his neighbour a part of the One. That is why his own global and unitive vision enables him to help and enlighten the other towards a possible integration with total unity.

What is the difference between the state of Samadhi *and realization?*

Roughly speaking the difference might be expressed

as follows, There is a state of consciousness of the Self which can be reached by a technique of relaxation of the mind. In such a case, the state of consciousness of the Self is what is usually called ecstasy or *Samadhi*. The drawback of such a state is that it may be both acquired and lost. As soon as the conditioning which in the first place caused the mind to relax ceases, one emerges from ecstasy and returns to the state of things which preceded it. Everybody knows the story which the Maharshi liked to tell, concerning a celebrated yogi who, being thirsty, sent his disciple to fill a jug in the Ganges. While waiting for his disciple, the yogi falls into *Samadhi*. During this time, the disciple goes to fetch the water, returns and sits down respectfully, waiting for his master to ask him for the drink, but the *Samadhi* persists. The disciple grows old and dies, two generations go by, and at last the master emerges from his *Samadhi*. As soon as he returns to the consciousness of manifestation. the first cry he utters is: "I'm thirsty".

This man had for many years been is a state of consciousness of the Self, but his state was conditioned by a voluntary technique of the stopping of the mind. Now every technique produces a conditioning; and no technique can produce a permanent conditioning because an absolute state of being cannot be a product. The *Samadhi* therefore had to come to an end and the yogi return to his former condition.

But that state of consciousness of the Self which is realization is something different. This state is not

84

really a state, it is a return to the natural original order *(Sahaja)*. This return is not reached by any conditioning. It comes about with the discrimination between the real and the unreal, with the elimination of the unreal.

This process of elimination is conducted as follows: one observes that one is in a world of impermanency, that one is immersed in the becoming process. The fundamental desire of the me being for perfect, that is permanent, joy, the first thing we do is to seek out an object, or a state of things which is likely to give us such joy. Sooner or later we come to acknowledge our failure. Such a failure if it does not lead to nihilistic despair can induce a turning back on oneself which may lead to the discovery of the Self. Such an experience of permanency, following on discrimination, does not take us out of one state to put us into another, it reinstates us in our original perspective, our vision. In such a vision, impermanency is neither conjured away nor veiled, but seen in its true light as an expression of the permanency of the Self. At this level, any opposition between being and becoming, permanency and impermanency, unity of the Self and multiplicity of objects ceases to be.

Meister Eckhart uses an image to describe such a state. He says it is like "the hinge which is motionless whilst the door turns".

9

Our talk today may cause reminiscences to occur. By this I mean that, as a result of our present reactions, certain moments of availability will appear in the course of the next few days, inciting us to dwell upon processes which we may have worked on before. Such moments will not be organised recurrences. Here there will be no discipline, or exercising of the will, but spontaneous moments when our approach will be more intimate. For in the course of these talks we may use words and expressions whose essence must be sought out, so that the whole of our being may be struck in its depth. Otherwise nothing would be left to us except purely intellectual accumulation which would only strengthen the ego. As long as the spiritual essence is not sufficiently decanted, perturbations, confusions and images (*Samskara*) may occur.

Words without the spirit that enforces them, are like residues which encumber the body undergoing fermentations. Once the disciple has understood the spirit of the word, he can peel the fruit and make use of it as he sees fit. We understand the true nature of an object when we see that it has no objective reality as such and is part of the nature of the subject. Such an understanding causes a progressive involution of that energy which had so far been invested outwardly in the object, and furthers the occurrence of eminently creative silences.

Question
Would you please outline for us the different stages of Sadhana, *and explain what is the realization of the Supreme, according to* Advaita?

Answer
Our establishment in our true nature is reached by a complete elimination of the world of objects.

Such authentic elimination can only be conducted in the following way. First of all, with the help of a teacher, one must understand that objects have no intrinsic reality and are nothing but projections of desire. This truth, when it is completely assimilated, produces a falling back of desire upon itself. That is to say, all the energy invested in the world of objects is now in a state of balance, of abeyance, of rest. This turning back upon itself of desire produces a stopping of the mind, and consequently an arising of the consciousness of the Self. This experience of the Supreme, discovered to be the very heart of our being, is the essence of realization. From then on, and always with the help of a teacher, the establishment in that state will be permanent.

As we have often said, this is not a passing state, but a permanent establishment in our true nature. It is a state of being which we only seem to have left, and which consequently we do not need to reach. The disciple then finds in the Self complete joy and no longer searches for it in objects which have no independent existence. Such is *Advaita*.

What is it that gives birth to desire which is the cause of pain?

It is our blindness as to our true nature which urges us to desire and this desire in its turn urges us to action. If we are to be free of desire, we must turn towards the unknown, i.e. "the subject which can never be an object". By doing so, we change the course of energy, which returns to a state of equilibrium, placing us in our original nature. We then rediscover the knowledge of our true nature.

As we can see, the path to the Self is completely the opposite of our ordinary analytical and objective knowledge by which objects are examined and submitted to our scrutiny. In passing we may note that even this ordinary knowledge is only objective when we no longer endeavour to grasp and seize. Emptiness, rest and relaxation further a state which allows truth to arise.

Thus it may be seen that any search, if it is to be fruitful, always requires the same fundamental attitude of deep, humble, choice-free listening. To return to the path of realization: having once known the experience, established as we are in the solitude of our absolute and non-dual nature, we can never again be subject to delusion. With the death of desire comes the vanishing of pain, since pain is nothing but a lack or a limitation.

Why are we not conscious of reality in the state of deep sleep, during the interval between two thoughts, or during a fainting fit?

We do in fact experience reality in these three states. But such an experience only leaves an impression of nothingness to our ordinary consciousness, because the state of consciousness which is then experienced is a purely objectless and formless one. Such a state of consciousness cannot be inserted into the framework of objective consciousness (which is with object and form) and it thus leaves an impression of blankness and void.

During the interval between two thoughts, is one conscious of a duration of time which might be prolonged?

The interval between two thoughts gives an impression of an extremely short stretch of time, but in reality, it is an experience of being beyond time. There is therefore no question of prolonging it. This question, like the one before it, comes from confusing the continuity of the eternal present with the discontinuous succession of phenomena.

How can we, with our minds as a starting point, realise our true nature?

By coming to realize that the subject-object, the thought-object of thought distinction, is not justified. Thought and the subject are of the same substance, the same reality. If we turn our attention towards the unknown, thought-objects are fused into substance-consciousness and the state of pure objectless consciousness may be realized.

Nowadays, much is said in psychotherapy of restructuration. What is your opinion of it?

The non-structured state is a state of decay and absence of co-ordination between the elements of the psyche. It is an essentially negative state. In order to be effective, a therapy must make use of the individual fancy of the subject and allow him to complement the existing negative elements in himself with other positive elements which he otherwise lacks. As you can see, this is not an analytical process, but a psycho-synthesis. A real restructuration can only occur when what is supremely positive (and which at the beginning is only an unknown something beyond the positive-negative duality) is visualised. If one proceeds in any other way, only a fragmentary and egotistical construction is obtained, and the person is still a prisoner of the vicious circle of his problems. But from the global point of view, there is no problem.

I was present at one of your talks in Turin when you spoke of attention without tension. May I ask you for a few practical hints on this subject?

This attention without tension is an extremely important factor for discrimination. On the psychological plane, we must cease intervening. At one and the same time, we must be receptive and active, free of the past, free of the future, listening only to ourselves and to he who teaches us. On the physical plane, one should come to a state where our muscles are devoid of attraction, devoid of repulsion.

We can easily notice how we are constantly on the defensive towards our surroundings and this state is a cause of disturbance, even physiologically. Both repulsions and attractions, with their trail of greed, trigger off impatience which creates a type of tension in our body. This state of constant strain often changes us into pitiful jerky puppets, subject to ridiculous tics. We should become aware of this state with a serene clear-sightedness absolutely free of guilt, merit or even any wish to change. Only then can that decisive reaction occur which may help us to break through our usual framework. One should thoroughly understand that fundamentally the body is nothing but idea. It is nothing but a bundle of ideas. These are crystallized, set and solidified by repetition and stagnation. The regeneration of the body may be obtained by a therapy which should employ the contrary process, establishing a discriminating attention which will dissolve and destroy all our set patterns. After all, the body is nothing but a collection of mental habits: the mind alone has produced them and the mind alone can destroy them by the reverse process. Such a process will allow us to acquire a regenerated, purified body.

I would like to make a few remarks about awareness. When we put ourselves in a state of attention without tension, a whole new range of sensations appears, each one with its own innumerable peculiarities. As a starting point, one should select that part of the body which, compared to all the others, appears to be most fluid, and light. Then one should intensify this fluidity as much as possible by widening it, and extending it slowly, progressively, patiently. This process leads to a general sensation of lightness in the body. In the end, we arrive at a feeling where there is no distinction between the body and the surrounding atmosphere. Essentially, this is a visualization, a creation of images which one seeks to make more and more subtle, light, unshaped, tending towards vacuity.

Very deeply embedded tension requires long and patient work at intense visualization, free from any striving, or any hurry, before it can be eliminated. One should evoke as many varied sensations, sounds, colours, scents and tastes as possible. Any sensation which is evoked and maintained in its state of original purity, i.e. independent of any association, of any memory, and above all of any appreciation, always produces a deep letting go. The greatest advantage of this method is that we arrive at a state of availability which favours discernment. For one should never forget that the impersonal experience occurs beyond any mental or physical framework. If we take a liking to such methods, we shall linger in a world of analysis and duality in which the mind indulges and takes pleasure.

What do you mean by mental activity? Does not the English word "mind", as is usually employed to translate the Sanskrit word "Manas", have a wider meaning than the French word "mental"?

Strictly speaking, in French, the word "mental" is a made-up word which is frequently used in Hindu circles as the equivalent of mind and *Manas*. One resorts to this word because the French language has no exact equivalent. I therefore employ the word "mental" to signify in a general way thought, imagination, will, reasoning, sensations, perception, and emotions. All this constitutes the ego, with its feeling of separate existence and identification with the mind-body.

The word "mental" is often used to indicate the domain which has been explored by western psychologists and which is often expressed by the word "psyche", so as to avoid metaphysical and religious inferences suggested by the word "soul".

You often talk of the orchestration of energies. By this word do you mean something akin to tantric methods?

Not at all. Tantric methods are voluntary disciplines whereas the orchestration of energies is in fact a letting go of the will. In our body there are networks of subtle energy which are revealed to consciousness when one has reached a vacant state. Such perceptions have hitherto been hindered by the presence of obstacles caused by strain and congestion. The Hindus use the word

Prana to indicate vital breath or subtle energy.

Vital energy has several different aspects which correspond to the different functional modifications of *Prana*. Among these aspects, one may mention:

Prana: breathing

Apana: excretion

Samana: digestion

Vyana: circulation

In ordinary man the energies unfold only according to a horizontal and descending pattern. Tantric techniques strive to change them into ascending movements, but these methods, instead of resulting in an establishment in the Self, in a real state of equilibrium, do nothing but accumulate these energies at a higher level where they are stored. Sooner or later a leakage may cause a collapse. This tantric search aims at a higher state on a physical plane, whereas *Advaita* by the method of discernment causes a reinstatement of the natural equilibrium of energies *(Sahaja)*. As long as the true nature of the object is not understood, energy cannot be kept in a state of equilibrium. Desire is always turned towards objects, thus giving birth to the cosmic process which can only come to an end with the understanding that bliss does not reside in objects.

When one is established in the background, how can one be simultaneously aware of oneself and of the object, since one cannot be simultaneously aware of several objects?

The Self is like a light whose rays are our mind and consequently the world. Beings and objects, under the most varied, the most heterogeneous aspects, are nothing but the fragmentation of the one and the same All, like the sparks thrown out by a fire or the web of a spider.

Each object is related to the background, consciousness. It should be understood that the content of consciousness is always necessarily a unity. In that sense it may be said that there is never more than one object present in consciousness at one and the same time, that is, present in the space-time sense. No two objects can be thought about together without being reduced to a unity. This unity is thus at each moment the object of consciousness. This is true when we distinguish between cause and effect. In reality, these two notions make up a whole, it is impossible to distinguish between corresponding notions. Cause and effect are grasped by the same act of consciousness and have an indissoluble unity.

The same is true of the idea of time. One may say, strictly speaking, that the idea of time is timeless. The idea of a succession implies that one seizes simultaneously and synthetically the different items of this succession. Otherwise, there would be a succession of ideas but not an idea of succession.

What is the mind?

In the dream as well as in the waking state, the mind is nothing but a function bred of desire. Silent plenitude precedes mental activity and follows it. The mind is nothing but an instrument of this fullness which it makes use of in order to act, just as we make use of our legs in order to walk.

Have the three states anything in common?

Mental activity and desire are active in the waking and in the dream states. In deep sleep desire and mental activity are suspended.

The common factor of these three states is the absence of the knowledge of the real. This knowledge of the real is not the knowledge of objects. It is only possible when the illusion of the me and of the world have disappeared. It must be thoroughly understood that all the aspects of multiplicity are superimpositions overlaying the Ultimate Reality and by which it is veiled. The vanishing of this superimposition reveals the truth which is then unmasked as is a shadow which one took to be a thief.

What difference is there between a mystic in the usual sense of the word and a realized man?

A mystic in the usual sense of the word is a man who seeks experiences and whose ideal is to reach a state of ecstasy. The search for ecstasy, for the experience of ecstasy, has nothing to do with realization. Ecstasy is a state – one can enter it and emerge from it – without having known any real transmutation.

The realized man on the other hand, has regained

the consciousness of his true nature, and is thereby reinstated in his primeval and eternal being.

The mystic, once he has emerged from his ecstasy, returns to his human nature, practically unchanged. He is in much the same situation as before and face to face with all the difficulties of life. Whereas for the realized man, the world has lost its objective and distinctive (consequently problematic) character, and then appears to him as shining forth from the Self.

I have listened to lectures on spiritual matters for many years, and yet I cannot attain the experience of the Self, and I am still obsessed by my problems. Do you think that I may one day be free?

This question is put by the non-Self. Now, a fragment can never have any notion of the whole. Eliminate the non-Self and what remains will establish you once and for all in joy and freedom. When one does not follow the direct path, one fails to see the chief problem, because one is absorbed by secondary problems, and one moves forever in a circle.

The fundamental problem arises from a mistaken identification with the body and the mind. All other problems stem from this one. When one ceases to cling to false values and when one clearly understands that the mind is incapable of grasping reality, one does not have the experience of the Self in the objective sense in which we understand this expression, but one is established in a state of being where all our problems leave us, just as a headache goes when we have hit upon the right cure.

Objective methods, although they are sometimes the cause of a certain opening out of the mind, shatter any chance of the experience which we are talking about.

In order to conduct an inner action on oneself I assume that one should be in a state of inner steadiness, in perfect health. Now I often spend restless and oppressive nights. Do you see how I could go about such a work on myself, a thing which I must do because I have a deep desire to find truth?

One must start from a certain number of given elements, and see what your present possibilities are. These possibilities can only be discovered in the fire of action, from moment to moment, and on condition that no judgement, no comparison with the state of your neighbour or the state you would like to be in, shall interfere. One must never be other than one is. If you follow this line of thought, you begin to feel yourself to be unique and that is what you are. By accepting your given state without any evasion, without any desire to escape, you begin to understand in a tangible way what you are capable of doing, and this understanding will act as a stimulant. By making the best of your present possibilities, which you fully know since you have completely accepted them, you will experience a blossoming which will be organic as well as psychological. Any other approach would be ill-timed and would only increase your impatience. From such a starting point you will respect both yourself and others, leaving all competitiveness behind you. This approach will show you your situation in society, with an entire certainty. It will give you a beneficial state of balance, a harmonious art of living. You will be at ease within the framework of your possibilities. Your deep desire to reach truth has given you a foretaste of it and you know that what you are searching for does not belong to the world of objects, but lies within yourself without any object.

As to the asthmatic condition I detect in you, you will cure it neither by allopathic nor by homeopathic treatment. Prepare yourself a better state of health by an adequate diet, chiefly composed of cereals and devoid of any acidity. Sugar should be particularly avoided and any recipes which make use of cooked fats. Asthma is a centripetal defensive and repressive reaction which stifles your physiology. It is a complaint entirely bred of fear; fear of an over-authoritive father, fear of tomorrow, of not being able to face certain situations, fear of losing one's capital, one's prestige, fear of loneliness, of death. With certain people whose entire personality circles around such a state of fear, things may come to such a point that, if the usual support accidentally disappears, they feel the absence of fear to be eminently uncomfortable and construct a new support for it. The fear of want is a thirst that can never be quenched, even if a man is satisfied to overflowing, for there is no such thing in this world as total security.

This satisfaction of a desire can provide us with a temporary satisfaction, but a new desire arises, directed towards another object, which no more than the first can give us a final gratification. Insecurity and impermanence are in the nature of things and that is the charm of life. Entire security only pertains to a state which is truly desireless. It is only when you come to understand with a total comprehension, that objects do not contain happiness, that you will suddenly find yourself in an immense void, where you can no longer refer to anything, and this state will give you a foretaste of a scented solitude. This silent fullness will never leave you, whatever the worries of the day may be. You will then have a new outlook on life, owing to your discrimination your energies will no longer be dictated to you by fear, and a marvellous sensation of expansion and liberation will take the place of oppression and stifling. You will then be cured at every level of your being and once and for all.

I am enslaved by so many bonds preventing me from leading this deeper life of which you speak, I feel tied hand and foot and quite helpless.

You are not free because you are convinced that you are your body and mind, whereas you are the ultimate knower. Foremost amongst these bonds are your thoughts. If you direct your attention towards the timeless reality, which understands these bonds, and not towards phenomena mistakenly taken to be objective, you will find that these bonds cease to be impediments. They are in fact nothing more than alarm signals which awaken you to a new outlook. Happy the man for whom the alarm signal sounds loudly.

I suppose that during the Sadhana *certain food should be avoided. Speaking as a medical man, I should like to know what you advise in the way of food which may help us to acquire this awareness and watchfulness.*

All acid foods should, I repeat, be avoided because they destroy the machine and empty it of its substance. All recipes containing fatty foods – and particularly when they are cooked – blunt and clog the physical body, preventing us from defining a problem with accuracy. Sugar in any form, with the exception of certain fruit taken with moderation, mollifies character, is a cause of laziness and wavering, leading one to avoid all problems, or put them off. Tobacco, alcohol and meat are stimulants causing heat, absent-mindedness and various perturbations which prevent the clear flow of discriminating thought. The most balanced diet is based on unrefined cereals. Of course all this is only a general guideline and should be adapted to individual cases.

In this path towards supreme introversion, what is the part played by the guru?

The guru being fully established in the background,

in the immovable Self is, according to the traditional expression, "the destroyer of darkness". His quality of spiritual teacher (*Acharya*) necessarily implies that he is able to determine the nature of the disciples' residues from the past and therefore provide him with the help which he requires. For him he unveils, one after the other, the various aspects of truth, and it is by listening to the teacher and afterwards to himself that the disciple gradually assimilates, with the help of meditation, the content of truth.

The teacher observes his disciple. He discovers the knots and diverted centres of energy, and when he realizes that there is no more antagonism and that the conflicts are sufficiently reduced, he intervenes and helps towards the realization of the experience.

This is the moment when the presence of the guru is essential. Once the experience has been lived, the final establishing in the experience will happen sooner or later. For he who has realized the Self, any feeling of personal qualification has completely disappeared and if he were suddenly asked who and what he is, he would just answer "I am".

The relationship between the master and his disciple is one of special intimacy. It is neither personal nor impersonal (in the conventional sense), but it has an incomparable character due to the fact that the guru, being established in the Self, is in fact the real "me" of the disciple. Thus it is said according to tradition, that the true guru is the guru in oneself.

I do not yet see very clearly how the teaching of the teacher acts on his disciple.

You must understand that the experience takes place beyond any mental framework. The disciple being always in an attitude of listening to his master who endeavours to make him understand what the Self cannot be, the disciple goes through a certain number of transformations and eliminations which finally leave him completely stripped. Later on, each time the disciple turns his thoughts towards non-duality, he will then go through the same set of eliminations each time with greater ease and less resistance. Finally, he will directly reach a state of plenitude; the final establishment in this state will then only be a question of time.

Do you think that religions have aimed at this establishment? And if so how did they proceed?

Sacred art by its very nature points towards the principle. Unfortunately, it began to disintegrate with the appearance of Gothic art and completely disappeared at the time of the Renaissance. From this time on, religious art lost its sacred character. The presence which one feels in a Norman church is already lost in Gothic buildings. The vertical striving which is their characteristic and which is usually felt to be so full of pathos and so specifically religious, is in fact an escape towards heights and indicates the disappearance of our feeling of the Divine in the centre of ourselves.

The Norman church by its very structure was for the believer an environment which could help him to enter into contact with his own divine centre. On the other hand, in a Baroque building, the divine presence is shattered by the multiplication of forms and colours which challenge the mind on all sides, excite and exalt it, but which entirely prevent any true meditation.

I know how interested you are in Indian music. It has remained truly sacred up till now because it has kept its traditional character, having always been transmitted from master to disciple. It is interesting to observe this mode of expression, where sound fills the dimension of sound space, ever returning to its centre, its fundamental point, the tonic. And the tambura with its four strings, the dominant sound being constantly heard, the superior tonic twice, and the inferior octave symbolizing the background, the Eternal Presence, while all the other instruments enjoy all possible development and variation. This reminds me of Goethe who, after having heard Bach's music for the first time, said: "This music makes us forget space and time, it would seem to be eternal harmony discoursing with itself".

Could you please reassure me that it is really because I forget my true nature that I am held a prisoner of the identification with a small myself considered to be active?

That which dwells in us and is conscious of our individual existence transcends it. What transcends this individual existence is our true nature which is never absent. The Self is beyond all our vicissitudes, beyond all the modifications of the three states, beyond birth and death.

Although we claim thoughts, sensations and emotions which constantly change as being our own, we are nevertheless not implicated in all this. The Self seems to take upon itself the characteristics of the individual (*jiva*) and the chain of causes and effects. From the human point of view, we have an identity which is expressed by the pronoun me and this me, the ego, is confused with the mind-body. The ego finds itself in the following situation: it may apprehend reality, i.e. return to the Self, or continue to identify itself with the mind-body considered to be active. But this identification is just a bad habit. We must become deeply conscious of it so as to free ourselves from it permanently.

If we cease to identify ourselves with any modification whatsoever, we are no longer affected by changes. One then understands that those objects which appear during the waking state or during dreams, are mere forms which are reabsorbed in the state of deep sleep. One then knows that one is the witness, the absolutely non-implicated Self and that objects can no more affect this witness than a lion in a dream can devour the dreamer.

But what happens to the world in all this? The divine game, the Lila of the Lord, in the positive sense in which Aurobindo uses the word?

He who aims at Ultimate Reality places no accent on the things of the world: it would seem completely futile to him since he has ascertained the unreality of things. He is more interested in the magician than in his enchantments and his achievements. The world is directed towards the perceiver, it celebrates the ultimate perceiver. He who is established in the Self is in no way interested in theologies and cosmologies. The construction of a cosmological hypothesis, such as the one which looks upon the world as a divine game, is a mental hypothesis due to ignorance, which does not understand the true nature of the Ultimate. The *Shastras*, and I am thinking more particularly of *Gaudapada*, assert that "Creation is of the very nature of the Shining One, for He only exists, He and no other".

Ultimate Reality is itself multiplicity, diversity. It is a waste of energy to strive to explain the world and its origin, which only diverts us from the essential Experience.

What is the ultimate state according to the Vedanta?

The ultimate state is a state where one distinguishes nothing, where one does not find oneself distinct. This state is a spontaneous realization of which one is aware, it is beyond any notion of distinction.

Printed in the United States
152463LV00002B/78/A